TRUTH ABOUT DIGITAL MARKETING: EFFECTIVE MARKETING IN 21ST CENTURY: DIGITAL AD

DISCLAIMER

Copyright © by H. HOYLES 2022. All rights reserved.

Before this document is duplicated or reproduced in any manner, the publisher's consent must be gained. Therefore, the contents within can neither be stored electronically, transferred, nor kept in a database. Neither in Part nor full can the document be copied, scanned, faxed, or retained without approval from the publisher or creator.

Truth About Digital Marketing

TABLE OF CONTENTS

DISCLAIMER

TABLE OF CONTENTS

INTRODUCTION

WHAT IS MARKETING?

DIGITAL MARKETING

WHY DO PEOPLE USE TWITTER?

INTRODUCTION TO SNAPCHAT

INTRODUCTION TO LINKEDIN

INTRODUCTION

This book is for every business man who recognizes the need of mastering digital marketing to stay current and who doesn't want to fall behind.
For every investor who spent numerous hours and a lot of money building their funnels but isn't getting the outcomes they were promised or knew were feasible.

For any manager who already feels like they are carrying the weight of the world on their shoulders and finds it difficult to imagine taking on any additional tasks.

H. HOYLES lifts the lid on precisely how to leverage digital to develop a magnetic marketing engine, increase business efficiency, and unleash unmatched development for your company in this open, conversational, and action-oriented book.

These things are revealed in this book:

WHAT IS MARKETING?
DIGITAL MARKETING
INTRODUCTION TO TWITTER MARKETING
INTRODUCTION TO SNAPCHAT MARKETING
INTRODUCTION TO LINKEDIN MARKETING

You need to approach your audience genuinely, think like a CEO, and be a digital marketing maverick if you want to rank among the best financial advisers in your field.

You may learn how to achieve it from THE TRUTH ABOUT DIGITAL MARKETING.

Do not fall behind.
Get off the hamster wheel of mass-produced advertisements and expensive fixes.
Unleash the potential of digital and alter the course of your company.

Truth About Digital Marketing

WHAT IS MARKETING?

In the beginning, the main goal of marketing was to use a set of techniques and strategies to sell a product or service.

Nowadays, it's not exclusively centered on achieving new sales. It's also focused on retaining customers, which means keeping clients who have already had an experience with the brand. Therefore, marketing now has two goals: attracting new customers with the promise of value, and retaining existing ones by increasing their satisfaction with the product or service provided.

So... How can we define Marketing?

We could say that marketing is the process or activity through which businesses, companies, and ventures implement different techniques and strategies to create, communicate, and exchange value offers with clients and partners, creating a relationship or instance of exchange that enriches both the client and the company.

Traditional Marketing

In traditional marketing, messages are addressed to the masses — that is, to a very large group of people. It does not allow for the detailed segmentation that is possible via social networks. Traditional marketing can be implemented by studying general aspects of the desired audience — for example, sex, location, salary, and other data.

This type of Marketing focuses on the 4 Ps: price, promotion, product, and place.

The message style is one-sided: you send a message, but do not have the possibility of receiving an immediate or interactive response from the client, so their role is passive.

These messages are promoted via mass media outlets (advertising on public roads, television, radio, cinema, etc.) to influence the purchasing behavior of the public. The ads appear in paid-for spaces in a specific location and time.

This type of marketing does not allow for the visualization of specific results and reports, although improvements may be seen after the campaign has ended. However, there is no definite way of knowing whether these improvements are actually due to the campaign.

Types of Traditional Marketing Strategies:
Outbound marketing is the traditional strategy for capturing customer attention with a product-focused message.

The message, along with the product information, reaches consumers who do not necessarily ask for it. Therefore, communication in this strategy is one-sided and impersonal.

DIGITAL MARKETING

We can define digital marketing as marketing actions and strategies carried out via digital channels and media. They can be purely advertorial or also commercial but are always carried out in a digital space.

In Digital Marketing, you can generate messages aimed at specific segments of people. In other words, you can establish differentiated messages for specific audiences with clear interests, tastes, and consumption habits, speaking to them directly and seeking a specific reaction or action.

Through this process, communication becomes bilateral and interactive, unlike in traditional Marketing. We can receive a direct response from customers, who now have an active role. This enables the creation of relationships and conversations between the company and customers, improving credibility.

In Digital Marketing we have the 4 Cs: Content (created based on select segments), Community (the human connections that are built through the exchange), Connection (updating content for each platform), and Conversation (constant feedback from the client).

Another important aspect of this strategy is that it is more profitable since we can alter our campaign at any time to achieve better results, without wasting any of the money allocated to the campaign.

In terms of measuring results, Digital Marketing allows businesses to access super-specific metrics. It is 100% measurable since it incorporates tools for calculating the effectiveness and scope of a campaign in real-time.

Types of Strategies:
Inbound marketing is a customer-focused strategy. Its first objective is to get to know the audience to which the product or service is directed and understand their needs, to look at how strategies can be adapted to these factors.

Communication is interactive and two-sided. The consumer is the most critical aspect, and all actions are based on them. However, this is not an invasive strategy (at least, it shouldn't be).

Evolution of Marketing

Digital Marketing began with the first websites, where messages were one-sided since there was no possibility of receiving messages or interaction from the public. Thanks to the creation of forums and the first social networks, what we understand today as online exchange began to occur. This had a somewhat revolutionary effect on the digital world, changing the focus of sales to customer satisfaction and loyalty.

Today, the user/client navigates this possibility of constant exchange in total comfort. Simultaneously, as technology continues to advance, algorithms and systems that store information about user navigation have become available, making it easier for platforms to provide users with advertisements for products or services that are in line with their tastes, consumption habits, or needs.

WHY DO PEOPLE USE TWITTER?

People use Twitter to find out what's happening in the world, get the latest news in real-time, exchange ideas with other people, brands, and celebrities worldwide, and be exposed to diverse voices.

The Power of Twitter's Audience
Twitter's persuasive crowd shapes the discussions that matter.

Leaders, Not Followers: They influence their friends and family.
#1 Platform for Discovery: Twitter is where people find out about new music, new technology, and new products.
Source of Information: People on Twitter are more open to your message. Most of them follow brands, so they're the first to know what's happening.

Start with them. Start with Twitter.

When people are on Twitter, they are ready to engage with you. Their minds are open. Their hearts are unlocked.

Why Should Brands Be on Twitter?
Twitter attracts an audience that wants to know what's happening.

On Twitter, brands can connect with a receptive, influential, and open-minded audience, which can help them achieve any goal they may have.

So, whether you are launching something new or joining the conversation, Twitter allows you to connect with the people at the center of what's happening.

When to Use Twitter

When launching something new, start with your Twitter audience.
Any new information you have to share with your audience is considered a Launch. This can include:

Brands
Products
Features
Messages
Promotions
Promotions

People use Twitter to discover what's new

How to Make Your Launch Worth Talking About
It's not just the reveal that matters. Today's leading brands build engagement using a phased approach.

Listen
Align existing consumer insight to your Twitter audience, or engage with Twitter to build a new audience insight.

Tease
Create buzz and awareness, and target a pool of influential early engagers.
Target the most influential users when they are more receptive.
Leverage content and formats that encourage sharing.

Reveal
Drive mass awareness of your launch to spark conversation and get your message through to the masses.
Use mass-reach products to break through and make an outsized impact on a large audience.

Reinforce

Reinforce your launch message after the reveal to drive preference and maintain buzz to keep your brand top-of-mind.

Consider multiple creative strategies to test and learn.

Re-engage viewers with downstream messaging.

Ad formats Twitter

Choose the best Twitter Ads Solutions for your goals

Twitter Ads offers 20+ product options to showcase your content and media in the best format possible.

Launch Creative Best Practices

Short and Focused

Keep promoted videos to 0:15 or less.
When possible, keep tweets < 50 characters.
Strong Visuals

Use captions and visual cues to get your message across without a sound.
Prominent Branding

Include clear and persistent branding throughout the ad.
Your logo should be in the upper left-hand corner.
Twitter is the best place to connect with what's happening.
Connect with:

Events: every event happening live on TV, such as the Oscars, the Grammys, the World Cup, any sports event, etc
Special Days: all those commercial or important cultural dates such as Mother's Day, Christmas, Cyber Monday, etc.
Trends: cultural movements, audience comments about your Brand, or anything that is happening in the world that everyone is talking about, such as #LunchAmerica, #Challenges, etc

Why It's So Important to Connect with What's Happening

People don't wake up thinking about your brand, so you need to make an effort to stay top-of-mind, by engaging with them through the things they are interested in.

Now more than ever, brands need to connect with what's happening

Source: Meaningful Brands Survey – Havas

How to Connect with What's Happening and Become Part of the Conversation

Planned

Foresee moments you know will happen, and produce content that will "feel" real-time when published at the right moment.

Anticipated

Create extensive lists of expected and potential moments related to the event.

Focusing on a few key moments and creating content that is relevant to them humanizes the Brand and makes the response seem "real-time."

Reactive

React to live conversations with content that reflects your brand's message or product set.

3 questions to ask:

Will it build relevance with your target audience?

Is there a direct connection to the Brand, category, sponsorship, or ad buy?

Will it help you steal a portion of your competitor's reach?

When Brands connect with what's happening on Twitter, they see positive results at every level of the funnel

INTRODUCTION TO SNAPCHAT

Snapchat is a camera and messaging app that allows people to connect with their friends and the world. With Snapchat, advertisers can reach a global audience and become part of their everyday conversations.

Why Snapchat?
Discover the Power of Snapchat

A camera to create and express your world — that's the power of Snapchat.
A Snap is much more than a simple text — it is a way to communicate and express your feelings with the people who matter the most to you, through your camera.

Real friends, real results. No public likes, comments, or pressure. You're free to be you, with the people you care about most.

How to Navigate Snapchat
The first thing you have to understand is that there's more to Snapchat than just photo and video messages that disappear.

In addition to the camera screen, the app has three main sections:
The Friends Screen
Swipe right for the messaging side of the app. Here is where Snapchatters chat with their friends.

Swipe up for Memories
Here is where you can rewatch your saved Snaps and Stories.

The Discover Screen
Swipe left to access our audience's main source of news and entertainment. Our Discover tab is loaded with stories from our community, content partners, and Snap's editorial team.

The Discover section showcases stories from sources ranging from mainstream media (The Wall Street Journal, Wired, National Geographic) to entertainment websites and Snapchat itself, which publishes curated collections of user-submitted Snaps related to certain topics.

The Discover section is also where our audience can view Stories from their friends, celebrities, and popular accounts.

To see less of a certain kind of Story, just press and hold it, then select "Hide".

Why does the camera matter?

Snap Audience

Snapchat is Growing Globally
Globally, 238 million Daily Active Users in Q1 2020, a 20% YoY increase.

Snapchatters are Actively Engaged
Having conversations with Real Friends is a Frequent Behavior.

Snapchat AR Generation
The generation that uses Snapchat's Augmented Reality is driving new behaviors and values that are changing today's world:

Meet the Snapchat Generation

The Snapchat Generation is increasingly becoming the most important generation for marketers to reach.
Why Is This?
Members of this generation are important to reach because they are still forming their brand preferences, and exploring the kinds of services and products they want to engage with and purchase. Also, they directly influence what their families are buying and spending time and money on. They are becoming the next decade's largest group of consumers.

Ad Formats

Discover the Different Types of Snapchat Ads Products:
Snap Ads
Make an impact

A Single Image or Video Ad is a full-screen ad that can be used for many objectives. Essentially add a connection and empower Snapchatters to swipe up and make a move.

Commercials

Engage your audience and drive brand awareness

Commercials are non-skippable for six seconds but can be up to three minutes long. These advertisements show up inside Snap's arranged substance.

*Not yet available outside the USA

Story Ads

Reach Snapchatters with a series of ads

Story Ads are branded tiles that live in Snapchat's Discover section. Generate excitement around your brand or latest collection with a series of 3-20 single image or video ads. This format is 100% optional for the user.

Collection Ads
Showcase a series of products

An Assortment Promotion highlights four tappable tiles to grandstand different items, giving Snapchatters a frictionless method for perusing and purchase.

Lenses AR Experiences
Create interactive moments with augmented reality experiences.

Lenses are a powerful and memorable way to connect with consumers using augmented reality. Create memorable, interactive moments that Snapchatters can play with and send to friends.

Filters
Take part in Snapchatters' conversations.

Channels are creative overlays that show up after you take a Snap and swipe left or right. Take part in Snapchatters' conversations as they visit neighborhoods, parks, restaurants, and shops, and celebrate important holidays.

Why Snap Ads?

1- Snapchatters

They are a unique, valuable audience that can't be reached anywhere else

2 – Their Power

Active Impressions

The reach provided by Snap Ads is active, not passive! Users are learning and creating, which means that every Lens impression is highly valuable.

Shared with Friends

Empower users to create on your Brand's behalf, and share content with their closest Friends, thereby building a community of highly devoted brand advocates. The power of influence of a friend is more than any influencer or ad could have.

3 – You will be able to Reach your Business Goals with Snapchat

Snapchat Ad products offer you the possibility to reach any marketing funnel goal — from awareness and consideration to conversions and responses.

Build Awareness
Educate Snapchatters on your business, brand, app, or product.

Build brand awareness
Introduce potential customers to your brand
Showcase new products or services to existing customers or potential customers
Drive Consideration
Encourage Snapchatters to learn more about your products or services.

Generate app installs
Increase website traffic
Drive engagement
Generate video views
Lead generation
Boost Conversions

Drive Snapchatters to take specific actions on your website or within your app

Increase website conversions
Drive catalog sales
Please note that Snap Pixel is required for conversion objectives.

Targeting Capabilities

You can set your ads to reach specific Snapchatters based on a variety of factors:
Interests and Behaviors
Reach Snapchatters based on the things they like and do — both on and off Snapchat.

Demographics
Reach Snapchatters by age, gender, or other demographic categories.

Location
Reach Snapchatters by country, location category (like "universities" or "beaches"), proximity to a specific address, and more.

Custom Audiences
Retarget Snapchatters who have already seen your ads or engaged with your business.

Lookalikes
Expand your reach by reaching new Snapchatters similar to your existing list of customers.

Brand Safety
Snapchat's mission is to build a trustworthy, healthy, and safe platform for Snapchatters.
That's why we work hard to maintain the privacy, safety, and well-being of Snapchatters and brand partners.

New products and features are developed with a focus on privacy and safety by design.
Measures are taken to protect our platform from fake news and misinformation.
Snapchatter data is treated with care and sensitivity.

INTRODUCTION TO LINKEDIN

For the first time in the history of the media, it is possible to reach professionals from all over the world in one place. As the world's largest community of business professionals, LinkedIn is the premier destination for finding and sharing professional content. Users on LinkedIn have a clear goal and a very different mindset and intention than those on other social media platforms.

Why LinkedIn?

The Right Audience
While LinkedIn has historically been leveraged as a talent solutions site, it has transitioned into a content-based site. 2 million publishers are posting fresh content on LinkedIn, along with peer posts in the Feed, long-form content, LinkedIn Groups, and 7 million brand-managed company pages. LinkedIn

is the definitive professional publishing platform, where members log on to learn, share, and get inspired.

Mission:

Connect the world's professionals to make them productive and successful

LinkedIn's professional environment is the only place where all of these audiences can be successfully reached:

Employees: who will become advocates for your reputation within their networks.
Customers: who will be vouching for your reputation with their wallets.
Stakeholders: who will be reacting to your reputation by way of stock prices and policy changes.
A Purpose-Oriented Mindset = greater ad receptiveness

Our Audience Sets Us Apart With Marketers

Data is up-to-date, accurate, and substantial, resulting in higher-quality leads.

LinkedIn Member Data:
Industry
Function
Company
Company Size
Occupation
Seniority
Title
Location
Connections
Group Membership

Marketers come to LinkedIn for our substantial first-party user data that is more accurate and highly differentiated from the market noise of audience data.

When you set up an ad campaign on LinkedIn, you have powerful choices when it comes to targeting your audience. You can target your content and message to over 706 million professionals based on characteristics like seniority, job function or title, company name, location, skills, industry, and more.

Additionally, you can take your first-party data and match it against the LinkedIn global member base to engage people even more likely to become quality leads. Combining LinkedIn and first-party data helps you target people who've already displayed an affinity for your brand.

Compared to other platforms, our data is more up-to-date, accurate, and substantial – the benefit of this is higher quality leads.

Advertising Product Solutions

Select Your Objective
Whatever your marketing objective, LinkedIn provides a full suite of products and features to allow you to reach your goals.

LinkedIn Audience

How LinkedIn Targeting Works
Targeting is a foundational element for running a successful advertising campaign — getting your

targeting right leads to higher engagement, and, ultimately, higher conversion rates.

What sets LinkedIn targeting apart from that of other platforms is that members are incentivized to keep their profiles accurate and up-to-date for networking, personal branding, and job opportunities. With LinkedIn, you can reach a quality audience consisting of influencers, decision-makers, and executives.

When members complete their LinkedIn profiles, they provide information on their job experiences, company, skills, and more.

This means you can target members using profile-based demographic information, re-target visitors from your website, or upload lists of contacts or companies for your account-based marketing efforts.

Tips for Optimizing Your Targeting Strategy
Now that you've found out about the various ways you can focus on your promotions in Mission Administrator, you'll need to know how you can advance your focusing on system to guarantee you're taking advantage of your missions.

Here are four important LinkedIn targeting dos and don'ts to get you started:

DO

Make sure your buyer personas are clear and well-defined.

Segment out key personas into separate campaigns, and group together the options that make sense, including related industries, locations, and job functions. This will help you deliver the right messaging to a specific subset of LinkedIn members.

Add no more than two additional targeting options in addition to the Location option.

We recommend the following audience sizes for LinkedIn's advertising products. Keep in mind, there's no one-size-fits-all recommendation, which is why testing is crucial.

Sponsored Content: 300,000+ members
Text Ads: between 60,000 and 400,000 members
Sponsored InMail: 100,000 or fewer member

DON'T
Hyper-target your campaigns.

It's tempting to use every targeting feature possible. However, a limited scale will hurt your campaigns.

Lump all of your buyer personas into one campaign.

You'll likely see poor campaign performance if you use just one campaign to target professionals in different countries, from different continents, and in unrelated industries and functions. If your target audiences are all lumped together, you'll have trouble personalizing your content for each stakeholder group.

More Customized Options with Matched Audiences
In addition to detailed Demographic Targeting, Matched Audiences also helps you engage those key accounts, prospects, and customers that matter most to your business, with:

Website Retargeting
Email contact Targeting
Account Targeting.

Using Audience Expansion and Lookalike Audiences to Reach Similar Audiences

Audience Expansion and Lookalike audiences deliver your content to members who are similar to your target audience in terms of Demographics and Interests. This increases the scale and reaches of your campaign by delivering your ad to additional members who may be interested in your content.

When to use Audience Expansion vs Lookalike audiences:

When you already have a high-performing audience – either from people visiting your website, people who provided you with their email, or a tailored account list, Lookalike audiences can help you find more people who look like these individuals or companies.

When you are using profile-based demographic targeting, Audience Expansion can help reach new audiences that fit your selected options.

Right Engagement

Companies with Completed and Active Pages are More Successful at Achieving Growth Objectives

LinkedIn Members Engage With An Investment Mindset
Professional network users connect with brands that align with their drive for success.

There are a variety of different needs and interests at the heart of personal and professional networks, and a variety of emotional drivers that fuel them. Marketing to the mindset is about understanding that mindset divide and aligning your marketing strategy to achieve the desired outcome. LinkedIn and TNS partnered to carry out a global study that surveyed 6,000+ social media users across 12 countries to uncover how marketers can connect to these different mindsets on personal and professional networks.

Personal networks are where people spend time being entertained, while professional networks are where people invest their time. Professional network users want to connect with brands that align with their drive for achievement and success. The type of content users expect from networks will align with their differences in personal mindset. In a ranking of the types of content users look for, "Brand updates" was ranked #2 for those using professional networks, and #9 on personal networks. Professional network users crave insight above all else and expect to hear from brands 26% more than on personal networks.

Members are here to invest their time. To achieve more meaningful engagement as a marketer, put yourself in their shoes and consider how to reach them with content that can help them develop their careers and better themselves.

How to Engage with Customers on LinkedIn

Awareness
Lead Generation
Consideration
Research

Right Environment

Our Environment Is More Trusted Than Other Social Platforms
LinkedIn is the most trusted social media platform and provides an environment that is conducive to building and owning your brand. When your audience trusts the platform (like they trust LinkedIn), they also are more receptive to brands they "meet" on LinkedIn (through organic or paid content).

We've got the right environment to drive trust, increase brand recall, and keep your business top-of-mind for users making business decisions.

Marketers navigating an environment in which consumer distrust is growing face the added complexities of fake news, ad fraud, brand safety, and declining media trust. Building the most trusted connections with customers requires rethinking media channels, communications, messages, and tactics.

Business Insider Intelligence surveyed 1,700 consumers to understand their perceptions of major digital platforms when it comes to 'legitimacy,' 'security' and 'community' in their digital media decisions. LinkedIn was found to be "undisputedly the most trusted platform." In their research, Business Insider Intelligence attributes this to the mindsets from which consumers approach different social platforms. LinkedIn's members approach the platform with a professional mindset, to inform and advance their careers. "This dynamic causes people to treat content and interactions on LinkedIn as more authentic," says Business Insider Intelligence, and in turn, "this engenders a higher degree of digital trust." LinkedIn is a highly trusted platform – comparable to other highly trusted platforms like The Wall Street Journal and Forbes.

Advertising Product Solutions – Ad Formats on LinkedIn

SPONSORED CONTENT

Build customer relationships at every step of the buying experience by targeting content to your most valuable audiences, wherever they spend their time.

Target your most valuable audiences using accurate, profile-based, first-party data

Reach your prospects anywhere: publish your content on the LinkedIn feed and in high-quality placements, for mobile and desktop

Grow your business at every stage: Drive quality leads, generate engagement, and raise brand awareness

There Are Three Different Formats for Sponsored Content:

Carousel

Single Image

Video

SPONSORED InMail
Send timely, convenient, and relevant private messages to the people who matter most to your business.

Sponsored InMail is the most direct way to engage with your prospects through LinkedIn.

Benefits:

Mobile-optimized design for easy clicks
Real-time delivery ensures timely reach
Uncluttered professional design
Flexibility for tailored content

TEXT ADS
Generate quality leads with an easy, self-service solution. Text ads appear just below the navigation bar on the home screen, as well as on profiles, pages, inboxes, and on network pages.

Easily create, manage, and optimize well-targeted, customized campaigns in just minutes – on a budget that works for you.

DYNAMIC ADS

LinkedIn Dynamic Ads is a personalized advertising solution that allows advertisers to accurately target decision-makers and influencers with highly relevant and customizable creative content on the platform.

Drive engagement with premium audiences using dynamically generated ads — powered by profile data, and customizable to meet your campaign objectives.

Build brand awareness by increasing Company Page followers and engagement:

Drive conversions with more clicks to your landing page, website, or app

Generate leads by promoting your LinkedIn content

From Brand Awareness to Lead Generation, marketers can reach their audiences on LinkedIn

Set up your LinkedIn Page

Start with a LinkedIn Page
LinkedIn Pages are a free and simple method for laying out your image on LinkedIn. All you need to get started is a LinkedIn account and a verified email address (we'll check to see if you're eligible to create a page on your company's behalf). Having a LinkedIn Page is required to run ads on LinkedIn.

There are more than 30 million Pages on LinkedIn. On the off chance that yours isn't one of them, you're botching valuable chances to get your substance before the crowd that makes the biggest difference to your business.

TO BE CONTINUED

www.ingramcontent.com/pod-product-compliance
Lightning Source LLC
Chambersburg PA
CBHW050315220526
45465CB00005B/2006